OXFORD STUDIES OF COMPOSERS

Skryabin

Hugh Macdonald

SKRYABIN

Oxford Studies of Composers

Oxford Studies of Composers (15)

SKRYABIN

HUGH MACDONALD

1978

London

OXFORD UNIVERSITY PRESS

NEW YORK   MELBOURNE

Oxford University Press, Walton Street, Oxford OX2 6DP

OXFORD LONDON GLASGOW NEW YORK
TORONTO MELBOURNE WELLINGTON CAPE TOWN
IBADAN NAIROBI DAR ES SALAAM LUSAKA
KUALA LUMPUR SINGAPORE JAKARTA HONG KONG TOKYO
DELHI BOMBAY CALCUTTA MADRAS KARACHI

ISBN 0 19 315438 2

*Printed and bound in Great Britain
at the Scolar Press Ltd, Ilkley, West Yorkshire*

CONTENTS

INTRODUCTORY

SKRYABIN is one of those few composers who made no attempt to be versatile, let alone universal. His first music was for the piano; later he moved into orchestral music, and he was content with these, the piano and the orchestra, for the rest of his life. The horizons of his art never widened. Instead they grew gradually and inexorably narrower, his gaze focused more and more closely on himself, and a clearer example of artistic monomania – in his case egomania – is not easy to find in the chronicles of music. This wholly inward-looking tendency is, of course, morally indefensible, and judging Skryabin's personality presents similar ethical difficulties to those we encounter when putting Wagner's equally self-centred behaviour in the scales. We are used to excusing Wagner's wickedness by referring to his music, or at least separating man and music into distinct compartments and discouraging our consciousness of one from affecting our judgement of the other. Skryabin, as a man, was a good deal less wicked than Wagner. He was extravagant and vain, he treated his first wife shamefully, and he depended for much of his career on the generosity of others. But he usually begged or accepted patronage from those, such as Belyayev and Kussevitsky, who stood to gain themselves, and he never flaunted hatred and ingratitude, as Wagner was wont to do. On the other hand the moral deficiencies of his character are not difficult to discern in the obsessive nature of his later music. The question then becomes: are these moral deficiencies reflected as artistic deficiencies?

It seems to me essential to view Skryabin's relatively small output of music as a whole. Not only that (and here another parallel with Wagner is evident), we should also see each work as contributing in a progressive process of growth towards some final achievement. This does not necessarily mean towards the final work; *Parsifal* is not the total culmination of Wagner, nor are the Op. 74 Preludes the summation of everything Skryabin did. I mean rather that each work is a link in a chain, or a brick in a wall. Early and late works illuminate each other, and in addition the early works are fulfilled and perfected by what came after. All his music shares idiom and gesture in a way that will strike many as repetitive. His musical vocabulary is narrow, but this enables us to grasp the nature and meaning of his musical utterance as though we could hold its entirety up for our inspection all at once. This oneness, this goal-seeking aspect is symbolized by the *Mystery*, a large, all-embracing work which Skryabin never lived to compose and which was essentially unattainable. It was to summarize, supplant even, everything he had written. More of the *Mystery* anon: in essentials it is useful in giving us (and him) a sense of a large dominant conception, transcendental and unimaginable in philosophical scope, of which the last works are mere fragments, sketches. I make no apology for regarding Skryabin's music as a progression in quality as well as in style. His brief career is constant development: his music gets ineluctably more sophisticated, more concentrated, more daring, more individual, more modern, more maniacal, and more profound.

Our purpose is to study Skryabin's music, but this cannot be done without reference to his character and background, especially since there is so marked a correlation between the development of his personality and the development of his style. The extraordinary flowering of the year 1903, for example, though explained in practical terms by his need to make money quickly, must also be seen in terms of the sharp change of direction that his life took at that time. The narrowing of his outlook, his total lack of interest in other men's music, his preoccupation with theosophy, his appalling self-delusion, these are obverse to the tightening of harmony and style which is gradually intensified until he created in his last music a totally private world. Not only was this development strikingly radical: it also took place in a remarkably short period. His transformation from a late nineteenth-century romantic, wedded to a sophisticated piano idiom, into a composer of the avant-garde who was regarded all over Europe, together with Strauss, as the spearhead of modernism (Schoenberg and Stravinsky were not yet seen in that light) took place in little more than twenty years. Skryabin died at the age of forty-three having already reached what might be seen as the giddy outer limits of a language he had forged himself.

Certain elements of his biography most pertinent to his music must be mentioned. The date of his birth, Christmas Day 1871, old style (6 January 1872, new style), was seen by Skryabin as a portent of his own messianic role. He inherited his musical gifts from his mother, an able pianist, who died when he was one, and not from his father, who was a member of an exclusively military and patriarchal family. He was brought up by an aunt, a grandmother, and a great-aunt, a female entourage which almost certainly turned his inclination towards the fastidiousness of later years, and since they spoiled him outrageously they may be responsible for his egomania and blind unconcern for others. He won easy access into Moscow musical circles and although his Conservatoire career was less brilliant than that of his fellow-student Rakhmaninov he never knew the true hardship of struggle or obscurity. It is characteristic that the severest set-back he did suffer as a young man was an injury to his right hand occasioned apparently by overdoing his practice. It cannot have been serious for he was soon playing Liszt's *Réminiscences de Don Juan* again, and yet the event was dramatized in the First Sonata by means of a Funeral March of deepest tragic tone. Skryabin was, like Wagner and Ravel, of diminutive height, and his hands were not big. This is of considerable importance when we consider the proper style of playing his music. He never played the Study Op. 65 No. 1 which demands a continuous stretch of a ninth in the right hand. He was nonetheless a formidable pianist even in a generation which produced such lions as Rakhmaninov, Lhévinne, Medtner, and Hofmann, and he gave recitals throughout his life.

His career was fostered first by Belyayev, from 1894 until his death in 1903, and from 1908 until 1913 by Kussevitsky. In 1897 he married Vera Ivanovna Issakovich, a pianist who doted on him and bore him four children. She continued to promote his music even after he had abandoned her (along with his teaching post at the Moscow Conservatoire) in 1903 for Tatyana Schloezer, by whom he had a son in 1908. Tatyana's influence strengthened Skryabin's leaning towards philosophical musing which dates from about 1902. At first his principal passion was Nietzsche, but in 1905 he encountered the theosophical teaching of Madame Blavatsky and Annie Besant, and his works assumed mystical significance expressed in fanciful titles or in poems and jottings which are best treated as profound or meaningless according to taste. Here is an example of one of these 'Promethean Fantasies':

I am God!
I am a nothing, a game, I am freedom, I am life,
I am a frontier, a peak.

Not only to teach have I come, but to love. I bring not truth but freedom. You heard my secret call, you hidden forces of life, and you arise; the waves of my being, light as a dream, arouse the world. To life, to light!
I awake you to life by my caresses, by the mysterious charm of my promises. I call you to life, hidden impulses which have perished in the chaos of perception. Rise up from the secret depths of the creative spirit!

It would be a pity if appreciation of the music required us to follow Skryabin into this world of cosmic hocus-pocus, but there will always be those who value the mystical element in his music as its prime virtue. There is a workable alternative: and that is to learn to distinguish the linguistic variations in his music in the broadest terms, that is to say, to identify the portrayal of dark and sinister forces, to perceive the music's constant tendency to take wing, Skryabin's love of fluttering, volatile figures, of trills and birdsong, and to mark the music's emotional intensity. There is also the pervasive erotic tone, a necessary adjunct to creativity in Skryabin's world. 'I wish I could possess the world as I possess a woman,' he once said, 'an ocean of cosmic love encloses the world and in the intoxicated waves of this ocean of bliss is felt the approach of the Final Act – the act of union between the Male-Creator and the Woman-World.' The final reunion of Spirit and Matter was to be achieved by means of art, in particular a fusion of arts. Skryabin approached this widening of his creative province from the passive end: his vision was of the senses all being gratified in a Final Mystery, a sacramental act wherein music, colour, and smell (ears, eyes, and nose), along with poetry, dancing, and gesture, were to be drawn together in the process of cosmic regeneration. In *Prometheus*, which springs from his preoccupation with creativity, he introduced a colour keyboard whose purpose is to envelop the listener in colour and light as the music proceeds.

Skryabin's fanatical devotion to these occult notions may seem extreme or even ludicrous, but it was wholly characteristic both of his age and of his nation. Apocalyptic writing was widespread in the early years of this century and the feeling of some momentous imminent event found expression in the writings of Blok, Ivanov, Merezhkovsky, and others, whether their inspiration was Marx, Wagner, Nietzsche or, more directly, Solovyov's prophecies of doom. Ecstasy and mystical love, the prime elements of Skryabin's imagery, were common currency, and when the great events actually arrived, war in 1914, and revolution in 1917, their significance was easily mistaken; Skryabin, who only lived to witness the first of these, welcomed it as a herald of a newly regenerated world, scarcely troubling to examine reality more closely than he needed. 'The masses need to be shaken. In this way they can be rendered perceptive of finer vibrations than usual. How deeply mistaken it is to view war merely as discord between nations.'

Skryabin also displayed a characteristically Russian tendency to pursue an idea, once embraced, with unswerving ardour. One thinks of Tolstoy's pursuit of peasanthood, the Soviet pursuit of Marxism, or, in music, Dargomyzhsky's pursuit of realism through unbroken recitative in his ill-fated *Stone Guest*. More moderate men would have stopped short of the mania that gripped all of these. But Skryabin's daemon drew him unrelentingly, and to that he owes both the obsessive sonorities of his music, his constant knocking on the same door, as well as the positive achievement of having attained a new and wholly modern musical style. Skryabin has often been considered as apart from Russian traditions, mainly because of his cosmopolitanism and because folk-song and the Russian nationalist school interested him so little. He resented this charge: 'Is it possible that I am not a Russian composer merely because I don't write overtures and capriccios on Russian themes?' The Russian inheritance is in any case plainly audible. If Chopin is the composer most obviously influential in the formation of Skryabin's early music, there are nonetheless numerous echoes of Tchaikovsky, especially in the first two symphonies. Where does the harmonic language of the opening bars of the Study Op. 8 No. 3 come from, if not from Tchaikovsky?

Ex. 1

The gloom of the close of the First Sonata is close to the gloom of the *Pathétique* symphony which it preceded by a year. If Tchaikovsky and Skryabin here make us feel the weight of private suffering, there is the yet more Russian capacity, expressed most powerfully by Mussorgsky in *Boris Godunov*, to express the burden of a whole country's woes, centuries of accumulated despair. Skryabin too, consciously or not, drew on this inheritance, first in the wonderful Prelude in C♯ minor, Op. 11 No. 10, and then more strongly in a later Prelude, Op. 51 No. 2, in A minor:

Ex. 2

Yet Skryabin was not himself gloomy by temperament; here he is reaching beyond himself to his deepest roots for inspiration. In his orchestration too Skryabin shows his kinship with other Russians. We hear pre-echoes of Rakhmaninov in the Piano Concerto Op. 20, and of *Petrushka* in *Prometheus*. He scores with intensity and a nervous edginess that recur in Prokofiev and Shostakovich. Furthermore he shares with Rimsky-Korsakov (though neither had much opinion of the other) a tendency to compose by cerebration, manipulating units of musical material from one pitch to another and constructing intricately organized patterns of sound.

His Russianness is inescapable, and certainly more significant than his cosmopolitanism, merely superficial when compared to that of Prokofiev or Stravinsky. Skryabin lived abroad for long periods and travelled widely, but he never fully absorbed any foreign cultures. Italian and French titles and descriptive fancies garnish the later music, but he only felt at home when writing and speaking in Russian. The great forces from outside Russia that stirred him most were Nietzsche and Wagner. These men built philosophical and musical structures which Skryabin aspired to emulate, but in his music Wagner's echo is only rarely found: perhaps there is a Meistersinger to be heard in the finale of the First Symphony, perhaps a reminiscence of *Tannhäuser* in the Prelude Op. 35 No. 2. Chopin and Liszt had much more to do with the formation of his musical style, especially Chopin. His music was Skryabin's bible. His rhythms, titles, figurations, and ornamental phrases all permeate the early works: preludes, studies, impromptus, and mazurkas were his favourite format. The key-scheme of his Twenty-four Preludes Op. 11 is the key-scheme of Chopin's Twenty-four Preludes Op. 28. Direct borrowings and imitations are frequent, for example the Nocturne (1884) from Chopin's Study Op. 10 No. 11, the Impromptu Op. 12 No. 2 from Chopin's Nocturne Op. 48 No. 1, the Prelude Op. 15 No. 3 from Chopin's Study Op. 10 No. 11. Many others could be cited. At all events the closeness to Chopin, for which Skryabin was inevitably taunted, declined after the first twenty-odd opus numbers, though it never entirely vanished. What Skryabin learned above all from Chopin was the easy manipulation of rich diatonic harmony infused with chromaticism. Any composer who built his harmonic language on seventh chords of all descriptions looked to Chopin for a model, and with it Skryabin assimilated the natural deployment of this harmonic language under the two hands, expressing it particularly in pianistic terms. Since Skryabin's development was to be so strongly harmonic in direction, Chopin's music remains at the core of everything he wrote. Here, in a passage from the Study Op. 42 No. 5 we see the wonderful sense of abandon and forward drive that can only have come from Chopin, a moment where Skryabin seems happy to cease to be truly himself:

Ex. 3

Liszt is less evident. Perhaps the volatile flickerings that become more and more obsessive in Skryabin spring from Liszt's Mephisto moods; perhaps the grossly overwritten sonorities of the Concert Allegro Op. 18 and the Fantasy Op. 28 inherit the textures of Liszt's orchestral transcriptions. But in his studies Skryabin's priorities are those of Chopin: musical utterance before pianism. Transcendental technique for its own sake never consumed him. He pursued the logic of cyclic construction in his symphonies and sonatas to the one-movement form, as Liszt had already done in his B minor Sonata and the symphonic poems, but by the 1890s cyclic devices were so normal as to have lost touch with Liszt's pioneering development of musical structure, not to mention Beethoven's. Few composers (prominent among them being Brahms) then dared to leave separate movements unrelated by thematic reference.

Other echoes in Skryabin's music should at least be mentioned, if only because he was so disinclined to acknowledge them himself. César Franck leaps from the second (più vivo) section of the Fantasy Op. 28 and again from the second movement of the Second Symphony. Franck's piano writing has much in common with Skryabin's. Grieg steals into the coda of the Sonata-Fantasy (1886), Brahms into the Preludes Op. 11 No. 7 and Op. 13 No. 5, Debussy (L'après-midi) into the first movement of the First Symphony. All these may be coincidences, for Skryabin's tastes were unabashedly narrow and his unconcern for other men's music soon became notorious. History repaid him by providing no composers to follow in his footsteps. He had few long-standing pupils and never contemplated the continuation of his own musical language without himself. Thus a number of composers dabbled in Skryabin's idiom in the period from 1910 to 1925 when his music was acclaimed everywhere, notably Prokofiev, Szymanowski, and Frank Bridge, and one or two cranks like Obukhov (who is said to have written his manuscripts in blood) inherited his messianic follies. But neo-classical reaction between the wars cast him into obscurity and disfavour and it was not until recently that his music has been reappraised in an atmosphere free of the incense that clouded the minds of his earliest admirers. Olivier Messiaen, after all, has inhabited the world of sensuality and mysticism in a strikingly similar manner; he too links colour, sound, and sense with an apocalyptic vision, and other comparisons may be made without assuming any direct influence. Skryabin's world effectively ended with his death on 27 April 1915.

Being confined almost entirely to works for piano solo and for orchestra, Skryabin's output is neatly classifiable. The five symphonies (stretching the term to include the *Poem of Ecstasy* and *Prometheus*) and the ten piano sonatas form a backbone, with many works in smaller format at all stages of his career. Other works are significant only by virtue of their misalliance with the rest: a Romance for horn and piano (1890), a variation on a Russian theme for string quartet contributed to a collective set put together by Belyayev (1899), a fragment from an unwritten opera (*Keistut i Birut*, 1891), and a little Romance for voice and piano composed in 1894 to his own poem.

Further aids to the study of Skryabin's music are its clear division into periods and the reliable chronology of the opus numbers. His early period is the longest, from the first surviving composition, a canon written when he was eleven, to the Second Symphony Op. 29 (1901), with the end of this period devoted to orchestral composition. The Fourth Sonata Op. 30 to the *Divine Poem* Op. 43 belong to a second period, covering the highly productive years 1902 and 1903. Two Poems Op. 44 to Two Pieces Op. 57 define a third period, around the *Poem of Ecstasy* Op. 54 (1905–8). The final period, springing from *Prometheus* Op. 60, goes from 1908 to 1913 with an additional group of prophetic pieces composed in the last two years of his life. These are not sufficient in number or scope to define another demarcation in his output, but they point tantalizingly to a new sound-world and to the long-heralded but never composed *Mystery*.

THE ALLEGRO APPASSIONATO OP. 4
FOUNDATION OF A STYLE

SKRYABIN'S career as a composer springs to life with one work, the piano sonata in E♭ minor written probably between 1887 and 1889. Here all at once is presented nearly every idiomatic feature of his first style in clear outline if not yet fully developed. Everything before it is trivial, derivative, and undistinguished (even the famous C♯ minor Study Op. 2 No. 1 of 1886), but here Skryabin is speaking with his own voice, an ambitious voice with the clear declaration that the impulse and the inspiration are there to be nourished. The sonata does not survive complete, both of the last two movements (of three) lacking short passages that can easily be reconstructed[1]; Skryabin published only the first movement under the title Allegro Appassionato Op. 4 in 1892, having revised certain passages. But the whole composition is complete enough and certainly good enough to warrant the designation 'oth Sonata'.

Without any ado (Skryabin rarely bothered with introductions) he plunges into a turbulent allegro:

Ex. 4

[1] Sabaneyev made a version in 1918; Roberto Szidon recorded his own in 1972.

First let us observe the key signature, E♭ minor. The nineteenth
century treated the remote key signatures as having special purposes,
especially D♭ major and G♭ major. For Skryabin G♭ major ceases to
be remote; it is normal, it is the very air he breathes, the assumption
being that his music sets off from a state of profundity and emotional
weight. We shall see how difficult Skryabin found it to compose in C
major. When it does occur in his early music, we wonder why. Its first
appearance was obligatory, in the Twenty-four Preludes Op. 11, one
in each of the major and minor keys, as in Chopin's preludes. It is
likely that Skryabin put the collection together transposing earlier
compositions into the keys he needed to fill (as Bach probably did for
his Forty-eight Preludes and Fugues), for we know that the Prelude
Op. 11 No. 4 in E minor was originally in B♭ minor. C major next
occurs in the fugue at the end of the First Symphony, one of the most
lamentable and uncharacteristic passages in his entire work. In the
Second Symphony, C major is for the first time given real significance,
for the finale is a resplendent march using a major transformation of
the gloomy C minor motto theme after the manner of Liszt and
Tchaikovsky. The feeling of emerging from the overfurnished

interiors of the 1890s into the glare of sunlight is unmistakable. The *Divine Poem*'s conclusion in C major is likewise to be regarded as a symbolic triumph of light over darkness. The *Poem of Ecstasy* was to end in a blaze of C major, and in what we must call the *Ecstasy* period C major came to be common in Skryabin's music, strange to say, as a preliminary to his abandonment of tonality altogether. But in the first two periods only three piano pieces are unequivocally in C: the obligatory member of the Op. 11 set of preludes is the first. The second is the curious Prelude Op. 31 No. 4 with its distinct sense of parody; the bland perfect cadence at the end has every mark of deliberate absurdity. And, thirdly, the Prelude Op. 33 No. 3, which concentrates more on its Neapolitan chord D♭ than on its tonic C.

The Allegro Appassionato Op. 4 in E♭ minor, the extreme key, is in 9/8, the extreme time-signature. Nothing could be more characteristic of Skryabin than his fondness for triple metric units. Nearly everything he wrote falls into groups of three. 3/4 and 6/8 abound, but 9/8 has the advantage of being triple at quaver and at pulse level. For Skryabin to confine himself almost exclusively to triple units was a further mark of his whole-hearted acceptance of romantic sentiment. Chopin, again, offered precedent enough. Skryabin's keys and metres may be linked by observing that common metres, 2/4 and 4/4, are as rare as C major. Loveliest of these unusual time-signatures is the second movement of the Third Sonata, the 'Intermezzo', with its graceful trio which retains the regular 2/4 pulse despite the ornamental triplet semiquavers in the texture. The real association of C major with common time is to be found in the finales of the first three symphonies and in the *Poem of Ecstasy*. Skryabin could hardly go further away from his elemental ground than this, and yet we can see how, in the finale of the *Divine Poem*, he was beginning to master what was plainly an unnatural manner of speech.

Triplets thus pervade every corner of Skryabin's music, and the fluidity and freedom of triplets will become more and more apparent. In the opening passage of the Allegro Appassionato they are used dynamically to drive the music forward in classic galloping style. These first sixteen bars (Ex. 4) illustrate another Skryabin fingerprint, which, being harmonic, becomes elaborately developed in the later music. It is important to note its presence here in his first mature work. The theme strides through the bass, as many Skryabin themes are wont to do, rising to C♭ in bar 2, to B♭ in bar 3, down further to A♮ in bar 4 and back to B♭ in bar 5. The harmony may be reduced as follows:

Ex. 5

The second and fourth bars are inversions of the German Sixth (a dominant seventh on C♭ in the key of E♭ minor or major). They fall either side of a tonic 6/4 chord, and their bass notes C♭ and A♮ enclose the dominant note B♭, a semitone either side. This pattern will recur time and again in Skryabin's music, especially approaching the dominant note from below:

Ex. 6

Let us look at some examples. There is a fine use of this in the third movement of the Third Sonata. Since these opening bars are some of the most exquisite in all Skryabin's music it is worth quoting the whole melody:

Ex. 7

The German Sixth occurs at (*x*), before resolving on to the 6/4 chord in the following bar. The Study Op. 8 No. 11 uses this harmonic switch with great delicacy and the Prelude Op. 15 No. 1 has a fine example, with the hint of a pause, before the 6/4 and the final brief cadence. A variation on the German Sixth is the so-called French Sixth, with its hint of whole-tone harmony:

Ex. 8

The very early Nocturne Op. 5 No. 1 has an example in its last bars, and it provides the *fff* climax of the third movement of the First Sonata, following a persistent German Sixth in the previous bar:

Ex. 9

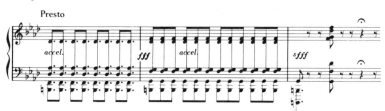

These few examples can only hint at the penetration of this kind of harmonic formation far into Skryabin's mature music. In the Allegro Appassionato the A♭ in the bass melody (bar 8 in Ex. 4) may sound momentarily uncharacteristic, but it is cancelled by the A♮ with its German Sixth at bar 13. The last two bars of that extract are wholly indebted to Chopin's kaleidoscopic chromatic cadences; such things were only to be found in Skryabin's earliest years.

The passage is repeated, but with modifications that lead to the relative major, and here the second subject is introduced immediately, presenting a total change of manner:

Allegro Appassionato Op. 4

(This is one of the passages most revised when the 0th Sonata became the Allegro Appassionato.) Both melody and harmony exemplify the sweetness which was natural to Skryabin but which he could also turn on artificially when required. Here its contrast with the opening is effective, its full extension making a completely satisfying section, as beautiful as anything in the early music, rivalled only by the third movement of the Third Sonata. Its naturalness is in contrast with the artificial brand of loveliness in the Mazurka Op. 25 No. 5 at the 'molto tranquillo', or perhaps also in the Study Op. 42 No. 4. In general Skryabin's lyrical gift was abundant, but his melodies are never independent of lush harmony, and his textures generally incorporate a pretended part-writing, as here.

Four elements of this second subject should be noted: first, in bar 16 of this passage there appears Skryabin's favourite 'horn-call' fingerprint, three stressed notes in the middle texture with no apparent melodic reference. It is the stress marks that hint at greater significance than one might suppose, and the significance is only elucidated by glancing forward at the way in which this sonority appears in later music. The best comparison is with the third movement of the Third Sonata (see bars 2 and 4 of Ex. 7) where a similar middle-voice entry is also stressed, though here the figure is doubled at the octave like a pair of horns.

These horn-calls have significance, not meaning; they are constantly close to the surface of Skryabin's mind and thus recur frequently. They seem also to relate to a second important element, the shape and spread of left-hand figurations:

Ex. 11

Allegro Appassionato Op. 4

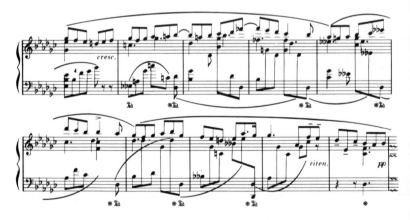

The link may be clarified if we first consider the Prelude Op. 13 No. 5 where the left hand uses the horn-call octave in arpeggiated form. Despite his small hands Skryabin liked to spread his arpeggiated left-hand figures high into the right-hand textures, as in Ex. 11, and this proliferates in his later music, arpeggios of seventh and tenth chords spreading both up and down through the texture. In the Prelude he seems to have deliberately modified his normal left-hand pattern to make the upper two notes of each figure into an octave leap, at least in the first few bars:

Ex. 12

Allegro

Prelude Op. 13 No. 5

The device is a conceit on the composer's part since the octaves are evident to the player's hand and the reader's eye, not to the listener's ear.

The third point may also be observed in Ex. 11 when a dominant pedal appears in the form of recurrent D♭s on the last quaver of each bar. When the spread figure continues in the beginning of each following bar, the effect is created of setting the bass note out of phase. We expect it on the first beat of each bar, but it arrives a quaver early. Such a dislocation of the bass note might be found in any nineteenth-century piano music, but in Skryabin's case it recurs often enough to merit special attention. It occurs particularly in the studies, a reminiscence possibly of the 'Paganini' episode in Schumann's *Carnaval*. Op. 42 No. 8 has both hands simultaneously out of phase and a constant five-against-three figure, leaving the listener entirely without metrical point of reference.

The fourth element to be noted is of fundamental importance, indeed it holds the key to our understanding of Skryabin, especially in his later music. Against the 6/8 flow of the music a number of cross-rhythms intrude, two against three, four against three and five against three. The contrast with the first subject, where the music has strong rhythmic drive, is complete, but it is not the tingle of cross-rhythm which we should experience; these free alternations are an attempt to notate a free-flowing texture in which rhythm has no exactitude. The two bars which precede the 6/8 time-change in Ex. 10 illustrate the point: Skryabin has seven notes to sound, two bars to sound them in. He chooses to put three in the first and four in the second, but he might have put a bracket round all seven over the two bars. At all events it would be absurd to play these notes accurately; they need simply to tumble forward into the new tempo. In his relaxed and languorous moods strict rhythm has no part to play; many wide chords have to be spread, and from that it is reasonable to assume that simpler chords should be spread too. The out-of-phase bass is simply a special case of rhythmic dislocation which allows time-values to vary freely. This style needs a continuous pulseless rubato; the music should be flabby, if such a word may be used without its pejorative tone, and improvisatory in feeling. The tyranny of a regular beat is undermined, and the harmonic and even philosophical aspects of this will become evident when we study the later music.

In the Allegro Appassionato Op. 4 it is more pertinent to see the free rhythmic style as a means of structural contrast, for the alternation of 9/8 drive with 6/8 relaxation provides a satisfctory if conventional formal outline. The movement employs regular sonata form as many of Skryabin's larger movements do; in his first period he was not making formal experiments, he generally employed a simple ternary form in the studies and mazurkas, while the preludes are much briefer. From his earliest years Skryabin showed a gift for the single brief utterance, an echo perhaps of Chopin's tiny preludes. The Op. 11 Preludes contain many good examples. No. 17 of the set has only twelve bars, the last four of which are a repeat of the previous four. Op. 16 No. 4 is an example of extreme concentration and economy, its twelve bars consisting of three-bar statement, first extension, second extension, and restatement, all in simple textures. This fondness for the briefest statement remained with Skryabin throughout and is still evident in the Op. 74 Preludes. In fact a preference for condensation rather than expansion is evident in nearly everything he wrote, the notable exceptions being the First Symphony and the *Mystery*, and in the latter case one may reasonably suspect that the problems of creating a work on so large a canvas would have remained insoluble.

One other feature of the Allegro Appassionato must be discussed at the outset, for it represents something deep-rooted in Skryabin's musical consciousness, something more elemental than a mannerism. It occurs here twice: the second time two bars before the cadenza, the first in the fourteenth bar of the development, and as it is its first appearance in his music, we must winkle it out of its hiding-place:

Ex. 13

The figure marked (*x*), with its characteristic trip, is like a written-out rubato, a light hesitation over the last of the three triplets. It is more a player's mannerism than a composer's. Yet Skryabin the composer absorbed this tripping phrase into his natural style and it recurs in all his music, variously elaborated. Its origin may well lie in Chopin, in, for example, the D♭ Nocturne Op. 27 No. 2 or the G minor Prelude Op. 28 No. 22; it is by no means uncommon in Chopin's right-hand decorations. In Skryabin it is omnipresent. Here are a few examples:

Ex. 14

Sonata (1887–9)

Study Op. 8 No. 12

Prelude Op. 11 No. 9

Prelude Op 11 No. 19

Prelude Op. 16 No. 4

Prelude Op. 27 No. 1

Examples such as these may be multiplied indefinitely, for it is basic to Skryabin's melodic thinking, especially when he is moving in triplets (which he generally is). But its occurrence in longer groupings – fours or fives or more – is to be noted, especially in a phrase which seems to tumble out of the sky, as in the example from the Fantasy Op. 28. It is a melodic tic, and in a large work such as the *Divine Poem* it may seem a deliberate structural unit when in fact it is no more than the composer's signature writ large. The rhythmic trip disappears from the very late works and is relatively scarce in the last sonatas.

Finally we may use Op. 4 to demonstrate the big, explosive piano style so loved by Skryabin and his contemporaries. The cadenza, the handfuls of arpeggios in both hands, the profusion of inner notes filling out the harmony and the massive dynamic requirements – all these are displayed in full panoply. They are demanded also in the First Sonata and in two works which give the appearance of being first and last movements of an incomplete sonata, the Concert Allegro Op. 18 and the Polonaise Op. 21, both in B♭ minor. The Fantasy Op. 28 also makes massive demands on the player. None of these may be thought of as good advertisements for Skryabin's gifts. Yet when he writes pieces that combine violence with brevity, the volcanic effect is highly original and telling. The Prelude Op. 11 No. 14, inspired by the sight of a mountain stream near Dresden crashing over rocky boulders, scarcely deviates from fortissimo or the tonic minor in a concentrated outburst of violence. The extraordinary ending of the placid Mazurka Op. 25 No. 6 is similarly explosive. Nonetheless for all their dynamic drive and pianistic satisfactions, these massive works lend weight to the suspicion that Skryabin was more individual and telling when speaking with a hushed voice, when delicacy supplanted bombast. At least this inflated style passed with his youth, and his mature music, no less virtuoso in outlook, pursues agility and delicacy in place of monumental grandeur. In any case the Op. 11 Preludes already revealed his gifts as a miniaturist and his impulse to condense his inspiration rather than to expand it.

TO THE ORCHESTRA

THE Concert Allegro Op. 18 was first performed by Skryabin in Paris on 15 January 1896. It is not difficult to see here signs of impatience with the piano's resources, and at least a determination to exploit them to their outer limits, nor is it surprising that he then took the decisive step into orchestral composition. This was to preoccupy him for the following six years. Piano pieces, some very fine – notably the Third Sonata – continued to be written, but the flow of miniatures – preludes and the like – is checked. This is also the period of his marriage and of his tenure of a teaching post at the Moscow Conservatoire. The familiar marks of academic self-consciousness, thematic rigour and organized counterpoint, are visible, but Skryabin's powerful drive towards experiment and innovation is by no means halted. Indeed these orchestral works were a necessary prelude to the *Divine Poem* of 1903, the work that turned the caterpillar into a chrysalis, just as the *Poem of Ecstasy* later turned the chrysalis into a butterfly. Significantly Op. 43 is entitled both Third Symphony and *Divine Poem*; it looks both ways, summing up the achievement of the first two symphonies and at the same time entering a new imaginative world.

Skryabin's first orchestral work was a Symphonic Allegro composed in a very brief period in the summer of 1896 while travelling in Europe. The full score was not published until 1949 and then under the misleading title Symphonic Poem, a title which Skryabin never gave it. Like the Concert Allegro Op. 18 it is a first movement without any movements to follow, probably an attempt to start a symphony. It is a dull movement in D minor, notable mainly for its opening theme's resemblance to that of the *Divine Poem*:

Ex. 15

Symphonic Allegro

Divine Poem Op. 43

It shows even more prominently than the first two symphonies Skryabin's too little variety of texture. It is not, on the other hand, pianistic in conception, it simply betrays the pianist's lack of imagination in orchestral usage, and the themes are too few to bear the repetition they suffer. Skryabin was doubtless fully aware of its shortcomings when he refused to publish it.

Unlike the Concert Allegro it is not bombastic, nor is the F♯ minor Piano Concerto Op. 20 that followed in the same year, 1896. Few piano concertos of that decade can emulate the restraint and finesse of Skryabin's concerto, three beautifully balanced, thematically unrelated movements, and the orchestral touch is already assured. In the first movement we hear the type of string melody against piano decoration that Rakhmaninov was to make his own, and his love of the clarinet as a solo instrument is unveiled in the slow movement, a set of variations in the tonic major on a divinely beautiful theme, a glimpse of heaven so unaffected and simple in style that one wonders how Skryabin failed ever to return to this uncharacteristic self-effacement (or to variation form either). The key of F♯ major provides at least part of the secret, for it has a similarly magical effect in the finale: the second theme appears, for the first time, very properly, in the relative major, A. But on its return in the tonic major, F♯, it has more than the mere tonal satisfaction of this perfectly regular scheme. By reaching F♯ it has reached the centre of Skryabin's universe:

Ex. 16

This may also serve as a useful example of a type of chordal melody that recurs often in Skryabin, where the right hand is in a cluster of three parts, the lower notes repeated not sustained. The Study Op. 8 No. 8 is another lovely example, both looking forward to its delicate use in *Fragility* Op. 51 No. 1 and, magnificently, in the main allegro of the Fifth Sonata. The different technical capacities of his two hands led Skryabin to write distinct textures characteristic of one or the other. This chordal right hand is a counterpart to the left hand's widespread arpeggios and the characteristic 'snatching bass' in the later music. The remarkable agility of his left hand was widely admired, yet, even if his right-hand technique was impeded by injury, the Piano Concerto, which he played frequently throughout his life, is evidence enough of virtuosity (for both hands) in the traditional sense.

The next orchestral work is a surprise since it is no more than a little piano prelude composed for orchestra. Belyayev gave it the title *Reverie* Op. 24, remarking that it was 'no longer than a bird's beak'. Rimsky-Korsakov thought it 'delightful, wreathed in piquant harmonies and not badly orchestrated'. The clarinet is again favoured, against the background of gently undulating strings that was to open the first two symphonies also, and a melancholy atmosphere hangs over these few pages. The *Reverie* is modest, but poetic, a tiny vessel that contains as much of the true Skryabin as the enormous hulk of the First Symphony, Skryabin's main preoccupation as the century turned. In truth the First Symphony is not vast on the Mahlerian scale, all six movements being short, but it aspires more than once to grandeur and attains only grandiloquence. The second subject of the second movement (which, since the first is a prologue, has the character and purpose of a normal first movement) suffers severe inflation at the end of the development, there are lapses of judgement in the otherwise lovely slow movement, and the last movement, the

29

epilogue, is a sad attempt to raise the work to a level of nobility which Skryabin could never achieve this way. It is a choral hymn to art, the only genuine stretch of vocal music he wrote, and although the solo sections have a certain repetitive simplicity, neither over-subtle nor over-plain, his choral writing is utterly characterless, especially after it modulates clumsily from the tonic E into C major for a fugue on the words 'Slava iskusstvu' ('Glory to art'). We may forgive Skryabin for thinking, at the age of twenty-eight, that his biggest work to date should be solemnly sanctified in this way, but it was not his best work by any means, and he mistook largeness of scale for profundity of utterance. These mistakes he was not to make again, for his orchestral works thereafter are more personal and concentrated (not actually shorter), and he left conventional rhetoric far behind.

There are many fine things to be admired in the First Symphony: the hazy opening, distantly prophesying the primordial beginning of *Prometheus*, the affectionate clarinet solos, the clinging harmonies in the strings over pedals on slow-moving bass-notes, the neatness of the fourth movement (the scherzo). The orchestra is not a large one: no percussion apart from the timpani and a glockenspiel in the scherzo, and a third flute and third clarinet. Enigmatically, the first solo clarinet is in A, the other two in B♭. All but the last movement are in triple rhythms, often with the rhythmic trip. Here and there a glimpse of his mature orchestral style emerges, in the harmony, the trills, or the orchestral colour, and that alone justifies regarding it as a prelude to better things to follow. Skryabin too felt that way. He wasted little time in embarking on a Second Symphony in C minor for the same orchestral forces, completed in 1901. Once again the finale presented a major problem, and although he did not ask for voices he strove to give the symphony a sense of finality and completeness by transforming the brooding C minor motto theme of the work into a brilliant C major march. It works no better here than in the similar passage at the end of Tchaikovsky's Fifth Symphony, and he later came to see this as the symphony's main weakness: 'Instead of translucence, which I wanted, I got stuck with a military parade.' There are not many other faults. The five cyclically linked movements, though longer in total than the First Symphony's six, are finely wrought, and he succeeds in the second movement in bringing off the most extended single musical unit he had yet attempted. Again it is the slow movements that touch the heart, the gloomy opening and especially the ravishing third movement, with its touches of birdsong and luscious harmonies, with strings divided into many parts. Again the harmonic rhythm is very slow; above a static bass the upper parts intertwine in chromatics he would later describe as 'parfumé':

Ex. 17

Second Symphony Op. 29

There is more imitative counterpoint in this work than in any of his others, and it doubtless cost him considerable effort, his musical sense being much more vertical than horizontal. Yet these passages generally flow well. They occur mainly in the opening two movements. This quasi-canon in the second movement would seem forced if the bassoons (and later horns) did not turn angular counterpoint into Skryabinic harmony:

Ex. 18

His fluency in triplet rhythms of every kind contributes much to the alert rhythmic drive of this movement. The 'tempestoso' fourth movement is even more vigorous, violent even, though the agitation is often more apparent than real, the bass note being firmly anchored while storms blow overhead.

The Second Symphony closes Skryabin's productive first period in a worthy manner. Were it not for the finale, it would be a great symphony. Skryabin is now speaking a language he is at home in and it is wholly his own; one might have expected him to develop the same vein much further, with complicated works in a recognizably contemporary idiom, sufficiently new to shock Arensky, Lyadov, and the old guard. But he did not rest there. The subsequent opus number, the Fourth Sonata Op. 30, breaks new ground, and so too, for all its similarities to the Second Symphony, does the *Divine Poem*, the Third Symphony. The orchestral outburst had given Skryabin the command of his materials to move forward from a position of strength; from now on he was truly a progressive composer, not just a modern one.

AROUND THE *DIVINE POEM*

THE *Divine Poem* dominates the period 1902 to 1904, years of profound change for Skryabin, in his life, his outlook, and his music. He had come to the conclusion that he should give up teaching at the Moscow Conservatoire and had found the work increasingly burdensome. His pupils were interesting and stimulating, but his work as a composer appealed to him more. Creative work is essentially selfish and Skryabin was a selfish man, though the decision entailed financial insecurity for some years. He had set his heart on living in Switzerland. Gradually a new pattern emerged. Two people close to him moved out of his life, two new ones moved in. In 1903 he met Tatyana Schloezer and, although he alternated between her and his wife for a year or two, Vera soon lost patience with the situation and returned to Moscow without him. Her refusal to grant Skryabin a divorce was a main reason for his long sojourn abroad, though even there, especially in New York in 1907, his liaison with Tatyana was liable to create difficulties with a whiff of scandal. Skryabin suffered greatly from this situation and neither relished nor flaunted it. His difficulties were compounded late in 1903 by the death of Belyayev, and though the firm continued to publish Skryabin's music, relations with the new management deteriorated, and payments were noticeably less generous. By good fortune Skryabin became the recipient of an annuity of 2,400 rubles from a wealthy young widow Margarita Morozova, a former pupil. Nonetheless he remained chronically short of money for many years.

Tatyana encouraged Skryabin's appetite for philosophy. From now on he began to write his ideas, disjointed though they were, in notebooks. He also planned an opera whose nameless hero was a Philosopher-Musician-Poet; where Wagner had embraced myth, Skryabin would create a philosophy-drama, presenting Schopenhauer's and Nietzsche's ideas of the Will leading to the hero's creation of a perfect world, fused with himself in a state of blissful ecstasy. It was to end in an extravagant Liebestod. The idea bore little relation to conventional opera and Skryabin encountered severe hurdles, worst of which was the failure of sung words to measure up to his unworldly ideals of expression. The First Symphony had already shown his impotence with vocal music. Music's capacity for rising above the involuntary precision of words can have few better illustrations than here, for Skryabin's music soars far above the ideas he attached to it. But he (or Tatyana) now saw every composition as the expression of his mental world and attached much importance to the meaning, whether mystical, philosophical, or fantastic, of each piece.

We see this clearly in the titles. The group of piano works that belong to this period (Op. 30 to Op. 43) includes for the first time six works with the title 'Poem', three of which are respectively titled *Tragic*, *Satanic*, and *Divine* (Opp. 34, 36, and 43). When the *Divine Poem* was first performed in Paris in 1905 it was accompanied by a lengthy explanatory programme, perhaps penned by Tatyana. The Fourth Sonata Op. 30, one of the masterpieces of the period, is accompanied by a poem about stars, mystery, desire, and flight; the *Tragic* and *Satanic Poems* had explicit interpretations. On a smaller scale these programmes take the form of directions in the music itself. The Fourth Sonata is the first work to bear these fanciful terms, such as 'quietissimo', 'rattenendo', and finally and very fittingly 'focosamente, giubiloso'. In other works 'fastoso', 'fermamente', 'elevato', 'agevole', 'vagamente' and other such Italian terms abound. In the *Divine Poem* Italian is mixed with French for the first time. Ernest Newman made fun of the direction 'Monstrueux, terrifiant' which appears against a 'clear little theme that is no more monstrous or terrifying than a white mouse'. Taneyev's comment to Skryabin was, 'You are the first composer who, instead of indicating the tempos, writes praise of his compositions', referring doubtless to the word 'sublime' in the slow movement of the *Divine Poem*.

It was meant as a jibe, but Taneyev did make the point that these terms are more than directions. They vary from instructions to the player, such as 'Comme un murmure confus' to programmatic footnotes, such as 'Ecroulement formidable' or 'Le rêve prend forme'. Many serve both purposes: 'avec une noble et joyeuse émotion' or 'avec une passion naissante'. Some are wonderfully poetic and suggestive. 'Très parfumé' (in the *Poem of Ecstasy*) is open to ridicule, but in its context it is evocative and right. 'Vague, indécis' suits its prelude (Op. 74 No. 4) perfectly. 'Légendaire', 'haletant' are marvellously apt; 'cristallin, perlé', in the *Poem-Nocturne* Op. 61, is superb. From 1903 to the end of his life Skryabin's music is studded with these imaginative labels, and they convey the atmosphere of each piece much more successfully than the poems or the notebooks.

New attitudes went hand in hand with a new style. The Fourth Sonata, in its very first bars, proclaims a new persona:

Ex. 19

The magnetism of fourth-built harmony is the most obvious element here, but its full development was to come later. What preoccupied Skryabin more at this stage was the general problem of tonality, a problem faced by all progressive composers of that date, particularly Schoenberg and Debussy. Skryabin still composes in fixed keys but the authority of the tonic is noticeably weakened.

The dilemma is evident in a number of ways. For one thing, Skryabin uses minor keys far less frequently. Traditionally minor keys provided the composer with more scope for chromaticism than the major, but Skryabin preferred to develop his chromatics within the framework of major tonality. The reason for this is evidently his preference for augmented harmony and for chords in which major thirds are prominent, but his way of explaining it was as follows:

'Minor keys must disappear from music, because art must be a festival. Minor is a whine. I can't stand whining. Tragedy is not in the minor key; minor is abnormal; minor is undertone. I deal in overtones.' There are minor key preludes in the sets Opp. 31 and 37, and in the Op. 42 Studies, but they are relatively few, and some of these, particularly the Op. 42 pieces, have an old-fashioned feeling; they may date from a few years previously. The Prelude Op. 31 No. 3 is incontrovertibly minor, thoroughly tonal and tragic in character, and the main C minor allegro of the *Divine Poem* is anything but a whine. The Prelude Op. 37 No. 1 in B♭ minor *is* a whine, but limpid and beautiful; the Prelude Op. 37 No. 4 in G minor is just a display of bad temper.

Skryabin still uses key signatures and concludes on tonic chords. The Prelude Op. 31 No. 1 is odd in having two keys, D♭ to start in and C to end in. In fact the form is neatly balanced since the first half moves from D♭ to G, the second from D♭ to C, but with an awkward twist in each half. For that matter the *Divine Poem* starts on, if not in, D♭ and concludes in C major.

The real sign of tonal insecurity is the way in which full cadences now sound awkward. The passage from the Fourth Sonata, above (Ex. 19), provides a fine example. The first eight bars manage to evade any tonal resolution, but the second eight, initially similar, deviate violently from the prevailing F♯ into a surprise B♭. Now the shift itself is not what causes an unsatisfactory moment, it is the full cadence in B♭. The more skilled he becomes at handling chromatic and extended harmony the more embarrassing are the triads; until he was able to eschew final cadences altogether Skryabin constantly drags his own music down by blatant moments such as this. A banal cadence weakens many works of this period, among which may be mentioned the Preludes Op. 33 No. 2 and Op. 39 No. 4. As the chromaticism increases, the cadences become more obvious. The *Reverie* Op. 49 No. 3 and the *Poem* Op. 52 No. 1 both end on tonic chords that have little relation to the pieces they conclude. Understandably it was a major step forward to conclude on any other harmony than the tonic, but he did finally achieve that in the *Enigma* Op. 52 No. 2, and, with a grand gesture of defiance, in the Fifth Sonata Op. 53.

To open a piece off-key was far less unconventional. Skryabin nearly always presented his main material in the first bar (the Piano Concerto is a rare exception). Furthermore he became fond, consciously or not, of making the opening phrase of a piece distinctly forbidding in outline; he liked to start well away from the tonic and work round to it. These three examples may suffice to illustrate the sense of *mediae res* imposed on opening gestures:

Ex. 20

Even the G♯ minor Waltz of 1886 had begun like this, with an unresolved discord. In the Fourth Sonata he combines an off-key opening with the languid, hazy feeling that so much of his slower music exudes, and once he had entered a harmonic land where cadences destroy the illusion of timelessness, the conflict between defined tonality and free chromaticism was hopelessly unbalanced. Divorce from tonality was already inevitable in Skryabin's development: triads henceforth have only a limited part to play, with a last defiant appearance at the close of *Prometheus*, when F♯ major steps across twenty minutes of turbulent chromatics.

Three harmonic fingerprints should be noted in this second phase. One of them is strongly diatonic in flavour, and often reinforces the tonality. It is the first inversion of a major seventh which for no clear reason appears in frequent alternation with the augmented and dominant seventh-based chords that surround it. This chord comes forcefully into prominence in the Fifth Sonata with the spectacular theme marked 'imperioso' and 'quasi trombe':

Ex. 21

(Presto con allegrezza)

quasi trombe
ff imperioso

It contributes a certain piquancy to the harmony of this period and the next, though the other two harmonic touches are more forward-looking. Both depend on the interval of the major third. We saw in the first period how Skryabin relied on the German Sixth to lead into dominant harmony, with less frequent use of the French Sixth. These were superseded by what we may call the Skryabin Sixth, since he made such a mannerism of it. In the same frame of reference as Exx. 6 and 8 the Skryabin Sixth has an E♮ where the German Sixth has D♯ and the French Sixth has D♮:

Ex. 22

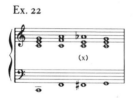

(x)

The Skryabin Sixth is no more than an augmented triad with one of the additional whole-tone intervals added. It thus has four inversions:

Ex. 23

This chord is unveiled with great solemnity at the start of the *Divine Poem* (see Ex. 15b above) and it comes in full splendour at the end of the first movement's exposition. Its more emphatic occurrence is at the end of pieces, notably at the close of the Fourth Sonata with the alternation of a Skryabin Sixth and the tonic, F♯ major, which may be reduced as follows:

The *Poem* Op. 32 No. 2 and the Prelude Op. 37 No. 2 have almost identical closes of this type. The *Satanic Poem* Op. 36 opens on a Skryabin Sixth and its colour dominates the whole piece. Consider both the first theme (in its inverted form) and the subsidiary theme:

Ex. 25   Satanic Poem Op. 36

The first of these two themes shows the third harmonic fingerprint to which attention must be drawn at this point. The three formations, German, French, and Skryabin Sixth, share three notes, C, F♯, and A♭, and are identifiable by the fourth note, respectively D♯, D♮, and E. The two fixed notes, F♯ and A♭, are not only regular constituents of Skryabin's vertical harmony, they also provide the two points of the scale to which his bass note tends to move. Tritone progressions become pervasive later, but the fall of a major third, from C to A♭, is already a mannerism. In Ex. 25a it is a fall from B♭ to G♭. It accounts for an occasional reminiscence of César Franck, as for example in the Second Symphony:

Ex. 26

Many other cases could be cited, and although these three harmonic tricks provided him with new vocabulary, they show too the tendency of his music to narrow, and to seem more and more made up of repeated patterns. Throughout his life, the resources he chose to use became fewer while his style simultaneously advanced.

The three masterworks of the second period are the Fourth Sonata Op. 30, the *Satanic Poem* Op. 36, and the *Divine Poem* Op. 43. To some extent he recaptured his feeling for the miniature, after working in orchestral forms for some time, but none of the 1903 preludes have the magical concentration of Op. 11 or Op. 74, which stand as models of the genre at the beginning and end of his career, the alpha and omega of piano preludes. The Studies Op. 42 seem less striking than the earlier set Op. 8, because they are generally more tonal than one would expect. They are no less taxing on the player. The breadth of expression in this period is widened, with the emergence of abrupt violent pieces and also of the languid style beautifully exemplified by the beginning of the Fourth Sonata (see Ex. 19), an ecstatic dream wherein the harmony seems to float, refusing to descend to mere earthly levels. Strictly speaking the sonata is in two movements, but they are continuous and the emergence of the opening rising fourths, *fff*, as the climax of the second movement no longer has the sense of obligatory cyclic transformation apparent in the first three sonatas. It emerges with the force of necessity from a brilliant build-up, and the sense of it being a one-movement sonata is inescapable. With the exception of the *Divine Poem* (already then in progress), Skryabin never again wrote in more than one movement, and the Fourth Sonata holds the key to this decisive step. Indeed it holds the key to the middle years as a whole, and it celebrates Skryabin's ecstatic feeling for F♯ major as no other work of his does.

Both the *Satanic Poem* and the *Divine Poem* are in C. The *Satanic Poem* is supposed to represent the devil mocking a pair of lovers, and his exultant power to destroy love. Uncharacteristically, Skryabin toned down certain interpretations in circulation: 'Everything in it is hypocritical and false. Satan is not really himself there. He's just a little devil, not in earnest. He's genteel and rather sweet.' There seems to be nothing malicious in the music, instead there is the constant ironic inflection, especially in the scherzo–like passages. Clearly the musical argument is based on the opposition of, among other things, the languid melody with a brisk scherzoso, the one marked 'amoroso', the other 'riso ironico'. But there is no suggestion of damnation or evil in these pages. It is, too, quite apart from its supposed diabolic significance, a fine virtuoso piece that Skryabin often played himself. The sonata form is wonderfully well integrated and rich in themes which take on each other's characteristics. Skryabin inverts his themes (in the first bar) (see Ex. 25a) and combines them:

Ex. 27

Satanic Poem Op. 36

The open fifth underpinning the third bar of this example bears Skryabin's unmistakable signature. Until the tritone came to be the basis of his harmonic style, the fifth often serves as an anchor under fluid harmonies, particularly, as here, when the root note, F, sounds beneath dominant harmony on C. Yet at the end of the *Satanic Poem* the tritone makes a powerful appearance providing G♭ and C as interchangeable bass notes, leading into the brilliant final close:

Ex. 28

The final cadence is, perhaps inevitably, a massive Skryabin Sixth hammered out before resolving on to C major.

The *Divine Poem* is also, despite its much greater length, intricately put together with related and altered themes that seem to grow out of one another. The three movements are continuous, they share their thematic material, and certain shapes and harmonies recur in many guises. Consider how the first theme of the allegro uses in its fifth and seventh bars an adaptation of the robust statement in the bass that opens the work (see also Ex. 15b above):

Ex. 29

and the same outline is used as a counterpoint to itself a few bars later:

Ex. 30

The slow movement's melody plays a part in the first movement's development, and the rising sixth on the trumpet acts as a repeated clarion call. It is an exceedingly intricate work, woven together with enormous patience and skill. Yet the effect, as Skryabin intended, is of unbridled sensuality, depicting spontaneous impulses and feelings. The title of the first movement, 'Luttes' (struggles), can scarcely encompass the range of feeling expressed in it, from the business-like main minor allegro music, to the warmth and passion of the sections marked 'avec abandon', where, over a firmly held bass note, the harmonies spread radiantly upwards. Then the development moves into prophecies of the convulsive, nervous music of *Prometheus*, and of the sinister forces already suggested in both of the first two symphonies. The dark, cavernous effect of stopped horns on isolated chords, and of six or eight low horns in unison, are set loose by the 'écroulement formidable' in the development, a passage where some kind of manic derangement or psychological storm invades the music. Yet there are also moments of calm and of Wagnerian placidity. One of the most remarkable passages occurs at the recapitulation when the main allegro theme is set against a subsidiary theme as a counterpoint in the bass, slipping into a 4/4 rhythm against the 3/4 pulse. A shadow is cast over the whole restatement.

'Voluptés' (pleasures) is at least an adequate title for the slow movement, in E major, which combines Skryabin's languid style with memories of the summer of 1903; the birds who sang in the Second Symphony return in full throat. Skryabin's neighbours in the woods of Obolenskoye were the Pasternaks, with thirteen-year-old Boris worshipping his idol Skryabin and dreaming of becoming a musician himself. 'Just as light and shadows alternated in the wood, and birds sang and fluttered from branch to branch, so fragments of the *Divine Poem*, being composed on a piano in the neighbouring house, carried and resounded through the wood.' That piano would not have conveyed the rich orchestration on which much of the movement's sensuality depends, with a solo violin and a few touches of glockenspiel for the more peaceful passages, and heavier intrusions from the full brass from time to time. The opening is elaborately scored for a small wind ensemble which gradually gathers in extra instruments as background for the violin solo, and the intensity of feeling is in constant flux. The trumpet's rising sixth peals out from time to time, and when the last movement arrives, this call turns out to be the opening thematic gesture. Skryabin cannot escape the necessity of C major and 4/4 time, but now he has learned to avoid the worst pitfalls, partly by lapsing into triplets whenever possible and partly by ridding himself of the desire to express nobility. Impulsiveness, neurosis, and unbridled emotional intensity served his purpose better, and chromatic elaboration saved the tonality from blandness. Cyclic references to the first movement close the symphony, and though the finale has at times more movement than momentum, it does not break the spell of the first two, and the effect of wholeness in the symphony is remarkably strong. Skryabin only solved the finale problem conclusively by never writing any finales again.

His orchestra is greatly expanded: four of each woodwind, eight horns, five trumpets, three trombones plus tuba, two harps, and strings divided frequently into many parts. His timpani writing remains little more adventurous than that of Haydn, and there are no cymbals or triangle, only a single stroke of the tamtam at the 'écroulement formidable' and the glockenspiel in the slow movement. Enormous orchestras were rapidly coming into vogue, and Skryabin delighted not only in the lushness and breadth of big orchestral sonority; he also began to exploit the intricacy and detail made available by a wide orchestral palette. This is discernible from time to time in the *Divine Poem*, although not yet so subtly developed as in his remaining orchestral music. Again, the workmanship is strikingly meticulous when we consider the need to harness intense emotional expression. Berlioz and Wagner both remarked on the exacting toil of composing highly emotional music: Rimsky-Korsakov had to apply the most mundane attention to devising his supernatural effects. Skryabin's passionately impulsive music is likewise the product of a lucid, down-to-earth mind, deluded perhaps as to its significance, but clearly focused and anything but deranged.

AROUND THE *POEM OF ECSTASY*

EVEN before the *Divine Poem* was published and performed in 1905 Skryabin was thinking ahead to his next orchestral work, his fourth symphony. The *Poem of Ecstasy* Op. 54 (which this became) occupied him for three years, the longest he ever devoted to the composition of a single work, and it was not completed until the beginning of 1908. As with the *Divine Poem* its composition was interleaved with the simultaneous composition of smaller piano pieces, Opp. 44 to 57; furthermore it too has a piano sonata, the Fifth, belonging chronologically and psychologically to it. Both Fourth and Fifth Sonatas are stylistically more advanced then their orchestral companions, and the kinship between the Fifth Sonata and the *Poem of Ecstasy* is closer than that between the Fourth Sonata and the *Divine Poem*, since a philosophical programme explicitly links them. 'Poem of Ecstasy' is actually the title of two works by Skryabin, a symphonic poem and a verse poem, the latter privately printed in Geneva in 1906, 369 lines of inflated mystical fantasizing of a kind familiar from the notebooks of this period. Skryabin devoted much of his time to philosophical study and dabbled in anything that mirrored, or seemed to mirror, his own ideas. He tried Marx, for example, and professed belief, but he preferred the theosophical teaching of Mme Blavatsky. His own incantations remained stubbornly self-centred:

I am freedom, I am life, I am a dream, I am weariness, I am unceasing burning desire, I am bliss, I am insane passion, I am nothing.
   I am play, I am freedom, I am life, I am a dream, I am weariness, I am feeling, I am the world. I am insane passion, I am wild flight. I am desire, I am light, I am creative ascent that tenderly caresses, that captivates, that sears, destroying, revivifying. I am raging torrents of unknown feelings. I am the frontier, I am the summit, I am nothing.

The recurrent notion that the world was his own creation and the hopelessly jumbled egomania of passages such as this indicate all too clearly how burdened and confused Skryabin was by his own creative gift. Its strength manifested itself in a stream of magnificent compositions but it also deluded him into thinking that the creative act was his own unique possession. He was not the author merely of his own music, but of all music and of all created things: he was, inevitably, God. The ecstatic quality of his creativity lies behind its self-indulgence and its obsessive depiction of 'volupté', 'délire', 'extase', and so forth; his head was turned by his own genius. But the saving truth lies in his recognition that philosophizing was not a necessary prelude to composition, but sprang out of it. His supreme musicianship generated absurd and, strictly speaking, redundant fantasies in words. One *Poem of Ecstasy* may safely be ignored: the other is a masterpiece of musical self-analysis. As Skryabin himself acknowledged, composing needed no outside stimulus, it was itself the fountainhead of knowledge.

He did not need to urge his muse forward, for the impulse to explore new paths was irresistible. We find in this group of compositions things that are startlingly new alongside echoes of his earlier styles, and the *Poem of Ecstasy* itself is a heterogeneous blend of the mature Skryabin with a more traditional tonal style. It is a transitional work springing from a transitional phase, the finest products of which are short, concentrated, and defiantly modern. The older elements of this period must be discussed first. Tonal feeling, for example, is still omnipresent despite the achievement of refusing in certain works to conclude on a tonal cadence. Strongest of all is the emergence of C major as a primal key. A great many works are at least nominally in C and his passion for F♯ is now less insistent; in fact only one piece, the Prelude Op. 48 No. 1, is unequivocally in F♯ major, and even here the Neapolitan chord of G is so evident that a cadence in C is never out of the question. Perhaps it was the phasing-out of key signatures that led Skryabin to adopt C as his favoured resting-place, though in more and more of these pieces the concluding tonality is not implicit in the work itself, and the weakness of insisting upon a tonal conclusion is all the greater. Two of the Op. 49 pieces, the Prelude (No. 2) and the *Reverie* (No. 3) suffer from weak final cadences. The Prelude Op. 56 No. 1 is the last piece in which a secure tonality really works, with the E♭ cadence implicit in the musical argument, not imposed on it. Tonal roots persist in other ways: one is the major seventh with its inversions, mentioned above (page 36). It is found in the *Poem of Ecstasy* (bar 9 for example) and plays a major part in the Fifth Sonata, though the smaller piano pieces rely on it less. The other is the increasing elaboration of dominant harmony over tonic bass, with its characteristic open fifth at the root of the chord. The *Fantasque Poem* Op. 45 No. 2 affords a good example in its second full bar:

Notice how this chord resolves abruptly on to a Skryabin Sixth in the following bar. The Study Op. 56 No. 4 and *Desire* Op. 57 No. 1 both end on such chords with no resolution:

Ex. 32

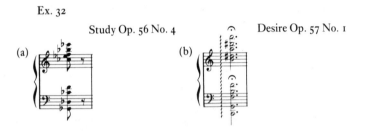

Study Op. 56 No. 4   Desire Op. 57 No. 1

(a)   (b)

These chords are always spread wide across the keyboard, to be freely arpeggiated, and their curious mixture of repose, generated by the open fifth, and instability, inherent in the contradictory elements above it, gives a particularly ambivalent flavour to this middle-period music.

In contrast Skryabin's increasing dependence on the tritone as the basis of his harmony pulls clearly away from the old functional harmony. Tritones had figured prominently in all his music in the harmonic texture; the Skryabin Sixth contains it. In the *Satanic Poem* Op. 36 (Ex. 28) we noted the appearance of a tritone in the bass, with G♭ and C providing alternative roots under a common harmony. Rimsky-Korsakov used the ambiguity of the tritone to superb effect in *Sheherezade*. Skryabin similarly relies on transforming a C chord into an F♯ chord with the minimum of effort:

Ex. 33

Unlike the normal dominant-to-tonic cadence these chords do not constitute a progression. The C chord does not lead into the F♯ chord; the dominant feeling of each is neutralized by its tritone twin. Gradually but surely Skryabin is undermining the horizontal implications of harmony, as Debussy did with his chains of parallel sevenths and ninths. The formal effects, for Skryabin, were far-reaching, as we shall see. For the moment Skryabin had the choice, when poised on a dominant-flavoured chord, either to resolve the bass by a fifth downwards, leaving the dominant variant unchanged, with a sense of partial repose, or to exchange the bass note with its tritone partner, producing the obverse of itself. More and more Skryabin chose the latter course.

The *Languid Poem* Op. 52 No. 3 provides an example short enough to quote in its entirety, and to examine in some detail:

The progressions in this piece, as in most Skryabin at this time, are of three main types. All the chords are root positions, so that one may extract the bass line alone to chart the course of the harmony as follows:

Ex. 35

The first progression illustrates the tritone alternation, significantly between the poles of C and F♯. The upper harmony is not much altered while the bass falls from C to F♯ and back again. Timelessness and languor are instantly conveyed. Tonic-under-dominant-harmony is shown in bar 3 and again in bars 9 and 10, prepared in each case by the dominant alone. The third typical progression here is the now familiar downward step of a major third, which happens four times. Particularly striking is the sequence from the C♯ in bar 4 to A in bar 5 and F♮ in bar 6. The one sequence in the piece which seems not to fit into Skryabin's world is the perfect cadence into the last bar.

This little piece also illustrates the subtlety of Skryabin's art as a miniaturist. In the middle of bar 4 there begins a sequence with, apparently, a two-bar phrase echoed at a higher pitch. At the same time there is a hint in the middle of bar 6 of a return to the beginning, with a tritone alternation and a shape very similar to that of the start. Yet no two phrases are the same; harmonies and intervals are altered, not transposed, and the whole piece grows outward from the middle of the keyboard to its outer reaches. This technical ingenuity is in fact masked by the overpowering sense of languor and heaviness that hangs over pieces like this, with the pulse very loosely defined. In twelve bars Skryabin's passionately indulgent nature is laid bare.

If we consider the *Poem of Ecstasy* after this finely wrought gem, the difference of scale is immediately apparent, although the tone of speech is much the same; in fact the ninth bar of the *Languid Poem* is close to the 'imperioso' trumpet theme in the *Poem of Ecstasy* in melodic outline. As we have seen, Skryabin at first contemplated a symphony, probably planned in four movements, and later spoke of it as 'Orgiastic Poem'. The verse *Poem of Ecstasy* was completed and published before the orchestral one and was not printed in the orchestral score. Skryabin's instructions were: 'Conductors who perform the work may always be told that explanatory comment is to be found there, but in general they should start by approaching it as pure music'.

Nevertheless it seems more constructive to consider the poem first so that those who wish to do so may pass on and dismiss its relevance to the music. The poem[1] tells of the spirit's search for ecstasy; its state of longing (the first theme is the 'longing' theme) is threatened by the 'terrible rhythms of dark presentiment' (Allegro non troppo, p. 22 of the Eulenburg miniature score). These are triumphantly overcome by the victory theme first heard on the trumpet (p. 24) and the spirit gives itself to the joys of love (p. 28, Moderato avec délice). The poem then has an inverted recapitulation not found in the music, a passage where the spirit is found discomfited and is revived by 'joyful rhythms'. The long passage in the poem recounting the struggle of the spirit between darkness and light clearly relates to the development section beginning with the Allegro dramatico (p. 49), and the poem has a recapitulation exactly equivalent to that of the music. The coda may be linked to the passage which concludes as follows:

> In this unceasing change
> In this aimless, divine flight
> The spirit recognizes itself
> As the might of the will,
> The single, free,
> Ever-creative,
> All-illumining,
> All-enlivening will,
> Wondrously playing
> In a multitude of forms.
> It recognizes itself
> As the trembling of life,
> As the desire for flowering,
> As the love-struggle.
> The playing spirit,
> The fluttering spirit,
> Creating ecstasy
> With the everlasting aspiration
> To give itself to the bliss of love.
> Amid the flowers of its creations
> It abides in freedom.

[1] The poem is published in English in *The Musical Times*, January 1972, pp. 26–7, and in Faubion Bowers's *Scriabin* (Tokyo, 1969), vol. 2, pp. 131–5.

The tone is precisely as ecstatic as that of the music, carried on almost blindly by a confused but powerful vision, and one scarcely needs to correlate words and music with any exactitude. It is probably more helpful to be aware simply of the labels Skryabin attached to individual themes. Theme (a) is a theme of longing, for example, theme (b) the dream theme, theme (c) the victory theme:

Ex. 36   Poem of Ecstasy Op. 54

These labels are hardly unexpected in the context of nineteenth-century programme music, so that the formal flux of the piece can be simply interpreted as the alternation of moods in the composer's mind. Above all the emotional intensity is unarguably ecstatic, whether languid and erotic, whether playful and volatile, or triumphant. The moods of the separate movements of the earlier symphonies have here been organized into a single movement so that changes of pace and character are very much more impulsive. But the formal outline of the *Poem of Ecstasy* is basically simple, on the lines of an extended symphonic movement. An introduction of eighteen bars presents two themes, one ((a) above) languid, the other (on the trumpet) marked with Skryabin's favourite term 'imperioso'. The lento (theme (b)) begins with the exposition proper in a manner very reminiscent of the *Reverie* Op. 24, with a clarinet sadly unfolding over a haze of strings. Subsidiary sections include the Allegro volando, fluttering and scherzo-like; another Lento; the galloping horns of 'dark presentiment'; the victory theme, (c), on the trumpet; and another passage, the 'rapture of love', rising 'avec une ivresse toujours croissante' to an ecstatic climax. There is a long development, a regular recapitulation and a long coda circling round and round the final tutti blaze of C major.

There was nothing new in compressing a symphony into one movement, and in Skryabin's case his impulse towards concentration had been evident from his earliest works. The artistic inflation so characteristic of the first decade of this century is nonetheless to be observed in the vast expansion of Skryabin's orchestral resources. The *Poem of Ecstasy*, it is true, requires an orchestra no greater than that of the *Divine Poem*, save for the addition of some extra percussion and the organ, but its vocabulary is incomparably richer and the intricate fragmentation of sonorities is greatly more advanced. One passage in particular seems to reveal the impact of Strauss's symphonic poems, when the conflict between darkness and light (the Allegro dramatico section) is enacted in orchestration of great force. Loud muted trombones dropping the interval of a seventh, chromatic scales boiling up from the depths of the strings, violently impulsive dynamics in the wind, all these were new sounds for Skryabin, and the skill and delicacy displayed, despite the enormity of his forces, is prophetic of the masterly orchestration of *Prometheus*. Some passages breed the suspicion that Skryabin had been listening to Debussy's *La Mer*.

I have heard the *Poem of Ecstasy* described as 'the obscenest piece of music ever written', said in approving rather than disapproving tones. Clearly it is not obscene; it will not deprave or corrupt. Skryabin's purpose is to inspire and uplift those for whom the ecstasy of creation is a comprehensible idea. The combination, or at least opposition, of languor and energetic movement may be overstated and the clangour of the close a trifle obvious, but it is a work of great strength, vitality, and originality. The inspiration is real and full-blooded. It is surpassed without doubt, by *Prometheus*, which is in every way a more consistent and single-minded work, yet it is the better known and more frequently played of the two works and will doubtless stand as a permanent illustration of the extreme height or depth (according to taste) which Skryabin's mind could attain.

The main by-product of the *Poem of Ecstasy* was the Fifth Sonata Op. 53. A superscription guides us to the point in the verse *Poem of Ecstasy* where it takes over from its orchestral counterpart:

> I call you to life,
> You hidden aspirations
> You, buried
> In the dark depths
> Of the creative spirit,
> You timorous
> Embryos of life
> I bring you
> Audacity!

There are no musical links between the two works, and the poem, an ecstatic hymn of love addressed to the world, i.e. Skryabin's own creation, can only be seen reflected in the music in its passionate, surging momentum. The Fifth Sonata is one of Skryabin's most athletic and mobile pieces. Its restless energy is almost unique in Skryabin. Yet the other extreme is not forgotten. There is a languid section in the introduction and a superb 'meno vivo' section (the third group of subjects) which simply oozes with the steamy, putrescent atmosphere so easily termed decadent:

Ex. 37

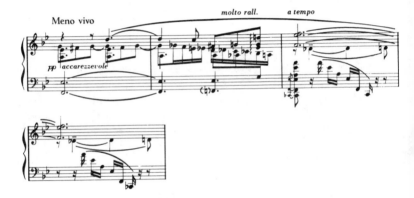

The sense of immobility and decay in this passage is overwhelming, even when at the end of the long development section it is built up into a climax of Lisztian grandeur. Slow drooping harmonies constantly interrupt the galloping pace and agile figuration of the main presto sections. Its sonata form is built on three subject-groups, a lengthy development and a regular recapitulation, with the most exceptional and striking passage coming first and last, an eruption of uncontrollable energy that rises out of the depths and vanishes into the top of the keyboard:

Ex. 38

The harmony of this first bar is not a random dissonance, as might be supposed; it is the superimposition of a tritone and a fifth used constantly in the later music in the low register as an exclusive left-hand formation.

The impact of this opening is just as strong when it recurs after the exposition, one tone higher, and stronger still at the end, since it closes the sonata in a series of explosions, each higher and louder than the last, none with any clearly defined tonality. In fact no tonality is ever established, despite the key signatures; E♭, towards which the closing pages gravitate, is the nearest to a magnetic centre, but Skryabin perceived, not a page too early, that his idiom no longer needed tonal resolution. The profusion of keys and of thematic material in the Fifth Sonata makes it one of the richest and least obsessive of his works, and its extrovert élan also differentiates it from the closed world of the smaller pieces and of the last sonatas. Invention and creativity were never so abundant.

Skryabin was now on the threshold of a style in which a sense of time had been attenuated almost out of existence. His music had never had strong momentum and his pulse had always been imprecise. Arpeggiated chords, a constant rubato, and frequent cross-rhythms were now supported by tritonal harmony that had no sense of forward progression. The music can hang timelessly in the air. Form is thus greatly weakened, for the idea of one bar succeeding another or of one chord succeeding another has less meaning. Instead of the dynamic, functional flow of traditional music, Skryabin explores the possibility of musical stasis, equivalent to an imaginary paradise of the senses beyond time. The languid style is the clearest illustration of this but it is no less obvious when the music *seems* to have mobility and pulse. Both right and left hands, in the piano music, have characteristic mannerisms to enliven the texture. The right-hand devices are trills, birdsong and decorative flutterings of every kind. The left hand often resorts to the 'snatching bass', which appears more and more frequently. It was already heard in the last movement of the Third Sonata (in the development) and in the Prelude Op. 31 No. 3. In the *Poem* Op. 44 No. 2 the left hand does little else, but Skryabin sees this left-hand idea as essentially violent, as the Prelude Op. 59 No. 2 proves. Activity without time is both a mystical and a musical goal which Skryabin pursues with relentless fervour, and his mature music gets as close to this quasi-religious ideal as the limitations of a merely human art-form allowed.

PROMETHEUS AND AFTER

IN the middle of the Fifth Sonata there appears in radiant colours the chord known as the Mystic Chord, whose fundamental constituents are the six notes (in ascending order) C, F♯, B♭, E, A, D, a chord analysable in a number of ways, like any complex harmony, but owing its special flavour to the tritone at its root and the group of fourths, pure and augmented, above. It is scarcely different from the tritone chords Skryabin had been using for some time and it is presented in many different guises, with extensions, alterations, and suspensions of many kinds. But it dominates the harmonic vocabulary of *Prometheus* and the last works, and deadens the forward flow associated with functional, tonal harmony of the classical heritage. Once harmonic progressions had been weakened, a much wider range of harmonic experiment became possible. In the Fifth Sonata, the chord appears thus:

Ex. 39

Prometheus, which Skryabin began to compose in the following year (1908), begins with the following chord:

Ex. 40

This is similar to Ex. 39 except that its lower members have been inverted and redistributed. The brooding effect of this chord dominates *Prometheus*, indeed it is often referred to as the Promethean chord, and it colours all the music of Skryabin's last years; mystic is not a bad epithet, especially with its unintentional suggestion of mist, since the harmony seems to float motionless, despite heaving and fluttering and recurrent attempts to animate this timeless music. *Prometheus* is not in any sense transitional; style and matter are one. The distance between *Prometheus* and the First Symphony, separated by only a decade, is immeasurable; they are scarcely recognizable as the work of the same composer.

In 1908 Skryabin began to compose what he believed to be part of the *Mystery* to which he had been making more than passing reference for a number of years, a large work which would unite the senses as

Wagner had attempted to unite the arts. He spoke of 'tactile symphonies', and of involving not just sound but sight, smell, feel, dance, décor, orchestra, piano, singers, light, sculpture, and colours. In the event light and colour were the only non-musical elements to be incorporated in this work and he was never precise about how touch and smell were to be handled, so to speak. His interest in colour stemmed from finding, in conversation with Rimsky-Korsakov in 1907, that they both associated colour with pitch, albeit different ones, and it is but one manifestation of the great surge of interest in synaesthesia which the European avant-garde displayed between Baudelaire and Rimbaud as its beginning and the triumphant progress of the cinema, with its total domination of visual media, as its end. Attempts to evoke the experience of one sense by an appeal to another were numerous. Musical images in poetry and painting were frequent; Whistler painted nocturnes, Debussy composed images, while the remoter fringe of synaesthetic experiment produced smell-keyboards and colour-organs against a background of limitless scientific optimism. The potential of these cranky machines seemed at least as great as that of type-writers and magic lanterns and other new-fangled fruits of mechanical ingenuity. Skryabin was not concerned with practicalities and had only the vaguest idea of what a colour organ could achieve. He simply believed that the experience of colour would enhance the experience of sound, as any devotee of psychedelia will agree, and he suggested that an audience will absorb the sense-experience of *Prometheus* more fully if it is bathed in coloured light corresponding throughout to the harmonic flow of the music.

The idea is unimpeachable and, on its own terms, correct, but the practical complications are severe. Skryabin never made any attempt to overcome them. To begin with, a large orchestra and chorus requires a large space in which to be heard, and no method of light-projection yet devised can bathe a large auditorium in colours which may change rapidly, many times in a single bar. Secondly, our aural perception of music is a great deal more advanced than our visual perception of colour, so that the simple reiteration of one colour every time a certain harmonic centre recurs has no dynamic value compared with that of music: steel-grey on page one is the same experience as steel-grey on page ten. The art of abstract colour in a time dimension has not even been developed by the cinema, so that in Skryabin's usage it is of an exceedingly primitive kind, whereas the music is exceedingly sophisticated. At all events critical response on those rare occasions in modern times when *Prometheus* has been performed with colour effects has noted the incapacity of changing colours, even of coloured shapes, to hold our attention for twenty minutes, as well as their incapacity to dominate the senses, given the economic and practical limitations within which experiment has been possible.

Skryabin's directions consist merely of the single stave of notated music marked 'Tastiéra per luce', light-keyboard; the music is in two parts, one part giving notes (colours) that change very slowly, ten times in all, each one lasting about two minutes. The second part reflects the harmonic patterns of the music, the note (colour) corresponding to the harmonic 'tonic' at any given moment, and so it changes constantly, sometimes very rapidly. Which colours correspond with which note was given by Sabaneyev (who knew Skryabin well) as follows:

C	red	F♯	bright blue
G	orange	D♭	violet
D	yellow	A♭	purple
A	green	E♭	steel
E	pale blue	B♭	steel
B	pale blue	F	dark red

Two notes are pale blue and two are steel (presumably metallic-grey), so that even if the harmonic root changes from, say, E♭ to B♭, the colour does not. The final chord, the only triad in the piece, is F♯ major, so that the *Poem of Fire*, as it is subtitled, ends in a blaze of bright blue.

Prometheus, the creator of mankind in Greek mythology, stole fire from heaven and gave it to the world. Skryabin naturally identified himself with such a figure, since all his delusions pointed to the world as his own creature. Where the *Poem of Ecstasy* dwelt on ecstatic sensual experience, *Prometheus* evokes ecstatic creative experience, both of course intimately related in Skryabin's cosmogony.[1] Nevertheless the two works are not easily differentiated in terms of content, except that the style of *Prometheus* is, as one might now have come to expect, a good deal more advanced and uncompromising than that of the *Poem of Ecstasy*. Its beginning paints the primeval condition of the world, before the first stirrings of life, before cries of exaltation or pain or love or hate had been heard. The choir, whose

---

[1] The creative flame is superbly depicted in Jean Delville's famous frontispiece to the full score of *Prometheus*, reproduced in Vol. X of the *New Oxford History of Music*.

wordless voice is heard in the closing pages, perhaps represents inarticulate humanity, but more probably they are merely a further sonority, with the organ and the solo piano, to add to the already vast range of orchestral sound. Skryabin's created world encompasses every timbre at his command and reaches out further to include light and colour. Colour, as we have seen, is only crudely applied, but instrumental 'colour' (the metaphor is here to stay) is as rich and varied as in any orchestral work of its time, even allowing for the orchestral excess everywhere evident in the years before 1914. The orchestra is again virtually the same as that of the *Divine Poem*, but its treatment is radically different. Sonority is much more fragmented; tiny details have proliferated while the harmonic pace has actually slowed down. In Strauss's *Heldenleben*, Schoenberg's *Gurrelieder*, and Ravel's *Daphnis et Chloé*, to name just three of *Prometheus*'s most advanced orchestral contemporaries, the same divergence between filigree of detail and breadth of movement is to be observed; abundant activity at the minutest level does not necessarily produce great momentum of the whole. In Skryabin's case this phenomenon of motionless movement, of busy immobility, contributes much to the character of the work.

The piece clearly begins with the birth of time itself, and concludes in (blue) flame, but in between its forward progress is slight. Like all Skryabin's one-movement forms, it has a clear pattern of re-capitulation but exposition and development here overlap. The music is episodic and repetitive, yet compact; form, being chronological, has little importance. As in the *Poem of Ecstasy* there is extreme contrast between the brisk, sparkling music in which the solo piano is prominent and the slow, heaving material, such as that of the opening bars. The themes do of course, develop, as for example the treatment of the first theme as something much grander than what may at first be supposed:

Ex. 41

Prometheus Op. 60

This theme is initially marked 'calme, recueilli', but later becomes 'thème large, majestueux' at figure 9 in the score. Consider, too, the contrast of the two bars marked, respectively, 'limpide' and 'sourd, menaçant', effected by a subtle shift of harmony and orchestration:

Ex. 42

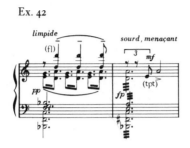

The tinkling, slithering, heaving, and fluttering depict a conception monstrous to some ears, masterly to others, but unarguably of superlative workmanship and extreme modernity, even for 1910, when the future of modern art seemed so rich. Its prophetic vision was crushed by events, and it became, instead, a symptom of decadence and excess to a world anxious to throw off its nineteenth-century inheritance.

After *Prometheus*, Skryabin composed only piano music, including the last five piano sonatas, written in the years 1911 to 1913. Each is self-contained in one movement, and each has its own character, yet they belong together as a group and form collectively an astonishing work of art. It is not presumptuous to compare them in this respect with the late Beethoven quartets, although their range of utterance is obviously and deliberately narrower. Skryabin, at forty, did not view these as late works; he looked forward impetuously to what would come after, and composed with ever greater fluency. With hindsight, though, they can be fairly judged as the summation of his creative life, of his piano style and of his pseudo-mystical outlook. They are more advanced in style than *Prometheus*, though many elements overlap. Each makes remarkable demands on player and listener; each combines a balanced musical form with a kind of timeless brevity and concentration (except perhaps the Eighth). In one other respect they may be compared to late Beethoven: a recurrent thematic shape is found in all of them, using major and minor thirds side by side. This was already present in *Prometheus*, whose first theme (Ex. 41) is an excellent illustration. Exx. 46, 47, 48, and 51 below are further examples, borrowing thematic shapes from each other (figure z).

Skryabin was also, as usual, composing much smaller pieces at the same time, the Two Pieces Op. 59 (the first tinkling, the second violent), the *Poem-Nocturne* Op. 61 (an oddity that seems close to the Sixth Sonata), *Mask* and *Strangeness* Op. 63, and the Three Studies Op. 65. This group of studies brings out the systematic element in his music since they exploit right-hand figures devoted, respectively, to ninths, major sevenths, and fifths. All are of course accommodated without difficulty in his harmonic scheme (with the possible exception of the second study, where the dissonant sevenths sound experimental) and the left hand is normal, with its tenths and tritones in all three. The third study is positively old-fashioned in style, with its enormous piano sonorities, tripping rhythms, and exuberant energy free of any brooding. *Mask* and *Strangeness* Op. 63 are superb miniatures, in simple symmetric form. Markings like 'bizarre' and 'avec une fausse douceur' hint at Skryabin's irony, but taken at face value these pieces are delicate, polished masterpieces.

When we come to the last five piano sonatas, Skryabin's own remarks are again not necessarily helpful. Between the Sixth and the Seventh, for example, he fixed a great gulf. The Sixth he dreaded and never played in public; the Seventh he adored, seeing it as sacerdotal in character, exorcising the demonic corruption of the Sixth and he subtitled it 'White Mass'. Yet the two works have much in common, in harmony, in figuration, and in form. Advanced tritonal harmony pervades both, and both use chord patterns as building blocks, 'Leitharmony' as it were. In the Sixth the recurrent harmony is presented melodically in the theme marked 'avec une chaleur contenue':

Ex. 43

The notes marked (*x*) define a five-note unit and appear on their own as the second subject with the marking 'le rêve prend forme (clarté, douceur, pureté)'. These five notes are often treated as a rapid, fluttering arpeggio, never as simultaneous harmony, although they give sharp, harmonic definition to the sonata. A similar role is played in the Seventh Sonata by a four-note harmony, two minor thirds separated by a fourth:

Ex. 44

(a)   (b)

Additional notes enrich this chord, especially the E♭, as at (b). These harmonic motives are the exclusive concern, in both sonatas, of the right hand. It is extraordinary how in Skryabin's late music the hands developed quite independent mannerisms without destroying the stylistic integrity of the music. The explanation lies in the fundamental deployment of the lower notes of his harmonic language in standard patterns of tritones, sevenths, and tenths, with an incidental fondness for the extremely harsh chord:

Ex. 45

while the right hand has freer choice in manipulating the upper elements of the harmony. It is the upper harmony and the right-hand patterns which determine the individual sound-worlds of each of the late sonatas.

Equivalent to Ex. 43 in the Seventh Sonata is the warm melody marked 'avec une céleste volupté':

Ex. 46

The major/minor-third Ur-thema (z) is again present here, as it is also in the Sixth Sonata when it occurs as an important regular counterpoint to the 'rêve' theme. The distinctive falling minor sixth labelled 'charmes' in the Sixth is parallel to the rising fifth, sometimes marked 'impérieux', in the Seventh. Both sonatas exploit grinding dissonances in the bass, of the types shown in Ex. 45, both have massive climaxes before the recapitulation, both have codas which reach into unsuspected thematic and textural territory, both have the high vertiginous chord-clusters, and the flickering, rippling arpeggios equivalent to phosphorescence or incandescence. But Skryabin was right to see the Sixth as a frightening work. Its streak of horror reaches a climax where he writes 'l'épouvante surgit' and there is a desperate release of power at the 'épanouissement de forces mystérieuses'. The coda is a violent whirlwind which even goes off the top of most keyboards, to high D. Its darkness is not penetrated even by the serenity of the dream music; the passage in the recapitulation, notated mostly on three staves, where 'tout devient charme et douceur' is a tour de force of complex counterpoint, wrapped in a dreamy haze. The same violent contrasts are felt in the Seventh, weighted more in favour of light than of darkness, of good rather than evil – to use Skryabin's imagery. Trills are more prominent.

The final three sonatas were composed and completed all at once, in the summer of 1913. Skryabin's inspiration was in full flood, though with little to spare for the preludes and poems that bespatter most other periods of his productive life. These three works are distinct in character and quality, though similar in being in one movement and in their general harmonic vocabulary. The Eighth is the longest, the Ninth the most concentrated, and the Tenth the most ethereal. The odd thing about the Eighth is that it has none of the concentration and brevity we have come to expect as Skryabin's hallmark; the themes and passages are spread thinly in plentiful repetition. It has its Leitharmony, presented in the opening chord, this time two major thirds and a minor third, and it has a somewhat tame chord-theme (at the first allegro) based on the single rising tone of the fifth bar. Development is mild but extensive, there are no violent climaxes, no threatening inner octaves, aggressive dissonance is suppressed, and there are scarcely any explicative markings so frequent in the other sonatas. Despite Skryabin's assertion that the falling shape in the third bar

Ex. 47

Eighth Sonata Op. 66

was 'the most tragic episode of my creative work', the Eighth Sonata is the lame duck in this final group, attractive and accessible, but without the compelling power of the others.

The Ninth is quite another matter, an unmistakable masterpiece. First let us note the Ur-thema, here marked 'mystérieusement murmuré':

Ex. 48

The unusual element of this theme is the series of repeated notes, a feature of great rarity in his music, and here used to brilliant effect, especially towards the end. Also unusual is the four-square pulse, with a 4/8 metre strictly laid out in pairs of notes: this truly makes its mark at the Alla Marcia section, in a pesante 4/4. The opening has the dry cerebral dexterity of Rimsky-Korsakov, with the left and right hands for once sharing the same music. Yet it is not mechanical in effect: the marking 'légendaire' superbly evokes the sense of a distant, mysterious wailing, which grows in force and menace and eventually tumbles in rapid cascades into the grotesque march. In the last seven bars it is pure desolation:

Ex. 49

The sonata has a distinct second subject ('avec une langueur naissante') frail and simple, but it has no recapitulation, at least not until the last line. Instead Skryabin builds a continuous structure of mounting complexity and tension. He pursues the combination of themes with unusual tenacity and eventually reaches a climax as harsh as anything in his music using a chord of two major thirds separated by a fourth:

Ex. 50

In 1916 Eaglefield Hull described the end as a 'characteristic
Skryabinic dance of cosmic atoms, mounting with ever-increasing
palpitation into a veritable molecular vertigo'. The atomic image is
fine, but rather than a whirlwind of fragments this sonata seems to
convey the concentration and explosive energy of a single nucleus. It
was not Skryabin but Podgayetsky who christened it the 'Black Mass'
sonata, but the title is scarcely appropriate.

The Tenth, like Beethoven's last piano sonata, is a trill sonata. From
the arresting moment on the second page when trills first appear, they
are never far from the surface of the music, culminating before the
recapitulation in massive handfuls battering at the top of the keyboard.
Towards the end the trills are laid to rest in a page of demented
twittering. The sonata is in superb formal balance, for the
recapitulation reverses the sequence of the opening, and leaves the
music suspended over the famous question mark of a falling fourth in
the bass. This is a sonata of craftsmanship and polish rather than an
expression of volcanic power. It is in triple metre throughout. In
contrast to the trills the opening has the obligatory theme made up of
major and minor thirds, and the main theme of the allegro is a kind of
melodic chromatic scale. Perhaps the key passage is the miraculous
four bars where the bass rests on fourths and the melody on major and
minor thirds:

Ex. 51   Tenth Sonata Op. 70

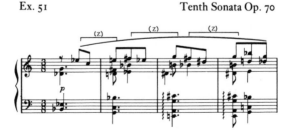

This is the supreme Skryabin: these four bars feel like a whole composition, so dense is the harmony and expression. It was the mysterious concentration of this style which provided Skryabin with the key to what was to be his final period.

TOWARDS THE *MYSTERY*

FOR the last two years of his life Skryabin worked on his long-cherished *Mystery*. He had been speaking of it openly for ten years and both the *Poem of Ecstasy* and *Prometheus* were, in a sense, premature attempts to bring this staggeringly ambitious conception to birth. In 1913 he again pronounced himself at work on it, but characteristically the plan was quickly modified so that the work in hand was not the *Mystery* itself but a 'Prefatory Action'. This was to have been a setting of a lengthy poem similar in style and content to the *Poem of Ecstasy*, except that the poem of the *Prefatory Action* was evidently designed to be sung. It exists in two versions, the second of which[1] marks off the sections that are to be sung by the choir and the various soloists, principally male and female voices, but also impersonations of the Wave, the Sunbeam, the Mountains, the Meadows, the Forest, and the Desert. The poem leaps from image to image, from dreams to fire, from ecstasy to death; angels, waves, flames and clouds mingle in an ecstatically sensuous outpouring, with a symbolic marriage of the Wave with the Sunbeam. But the poem actually says very little; words and images are there for their symbolic and sensuous appeal; no great mystical truth has been divined, no great philosophical issue engaged.

In all probability Skryabin knew full well how ill-equipped he was to set words to music; the First Symphony offered no encouragement

---

[1] A translation, by George Reavey, is given in Faubion Bowers's *Scriabin*, vol. 2, pp. 271–6.

and his style was anything but vocal. So we find among the fifty-odd pages of sketches of the *Prefatory Action* which have survived no trace of vocal settings, but simply musical jottings in a very incomplete state.[1] The most interesting aspect of these sketches is Skryabin's preoccupation with twelve-note chords, using every note of the chromatic scale in simultaneous harmony, an advance first made by Berg (unknown to Skryabin) in 1912. Complex though Skryabin's harmony was, this was an extraordinary forward leap for his music to take, perhaps the longest of many astounding leaps in his short career.

The sketches also contain a fragmentary citation of one of the few short piano pieces whose composition dates from the same last two years of his life and which give us the only other glimpse of what Skryabin's style might eventually have become. After the Tenth Sonata Op. 70, he published the *Two Poems* Op. 71, *Towards the Flame* Op. 72, Two Dances Op. 73, and Five Preludes Op. 74. Most of these pieces show a clear new direction in style, though three belong still to the fully mature style of *Prometheus* and the last sonatas: the second *Poem* of Op. 71, *Towards the Flame* Op. 72 and *Dark Flames* Op. 73 No. 1. On the other hand the first real specimen of the final manner is a little earlier, being the Prelude Op. 67 No. 1. This piece is 'vague, mystérieux'; the harmony is harsh but muted and it wanders aimlessly, scarcely rising above pianissimo for thirty-five bars, never altering in texture of tempo save for an impulsive burst of speed at the end. It is impenetrable yet profound. *Towards the Flame* Op. 72 is unique in Skryabin's piano music in its unmistakably orchestral sonority, indeed it was originally intended for orchestra before being planned as a sonata and then finally as a detached piece. It is also unique in being a general crescendo from beginning to end with scarcely any melodic content beyond the endless drop of a semitone (sometimes a tone) and it closes in a blaze of E major. Could Skryabin have really seen this tonality as pale blue? The flame should have been C major red.

The ultimate Skryabin is reached in the five short Preludes Op. 74, supposedly sketches or fragments of the *Prefatory Action*, and thus of the *Mystery*. Not for the first time he composed music that was at once experimental and masterly. While No. 4 is the most prophetic, being

---

[1] A work recently recorded in the USSR under the title *Universe* is described as the *Prefatory Action* in a reconstruction by the Soviet composer Nemtin. It is a magnificent work of pastiche using elements from the sketches and revealing an uncanny gift for reproducing Skryabin's mature style, but it cannot claim to be the work Skryabin would have composed.

close to the atonal style of Berg, and while No. 2 – slow wailing chromatics over an ostinato – was Skryabin's own favourite, No. 1 is surely the greatest of the set. It is also the shortest, with a concentration familiar from as far back as Op. 11. But the feverish power of every piercing dissonance is not even captured by Skryabin's own marking 'Douloureux, déchirant':

Ex. 52   Prelude Op. 74 No. 1

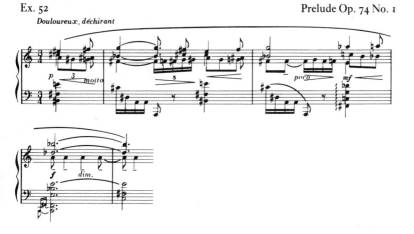

The inner harmonies tear at the music until near breaking point. The old tritone harmony, the composer's signature, still peeps through, but the clashing of upper parts is flagrant modernism of a most uncompromising kind. How paltry are Skryabin's own verses in the poem of the *Prefatory Action* when we compare them to the strength of utterances such as these! Beethoven, whom Skryabin so despised, could match the density of this music, but few others, not even Schoenberg in his own short piano pieces of a few years later.

Skryabin died in April 1915, with his life's work far from complete. It is tempting to speculate on the phase he was then moving into, the direction his music might have taken and the achievement he might have boasted. What would the *Mystery* have been like? Would he have evolved a serial technique? Such questions are fundamentally unanswerable since it is an artist's prerogative to defy expectation, otherwise his genius would be predictable and therefore uninteresting. Yet, given the works he did complete, their styles, their tendency to concentration and his ever narrower and more egocentric outlook, it is virtually impossible to imagine how a large-scale work for orchestra, voices, dancers, and ritual could ever have been written. Humanity at large had almost ceased to exist for him. The kinds of matter which most composers encompass – heroism, national fervour, religious ritual, human love, not to mention time-honoured musical principles such as concerto or fugue – were totally excluded from his imaginative world. He could expand his language by advancing in style and technique but not by moving outwards away from himself. He lived in a mirrored gallery of tiny dimension where his own image seemed to him to stretch far in every direction. He lacked common humanity as a man and universality as a musician. He was monarch of all he surveyed, deluded into believing that what he surveyed was the universe itself.

Why then is his music so satisfying if points of contact with other human beings were so scanty? Do we not need to recognize a shared humanity in a work of art? If Skryabin had worked in a representational art-form his work would be worthless, as his poems and his settings of words confirm. It is because his music can signify things other than those imagined by the composer that we can accept that the music is, for example, beautiful and expressive, not necessarily expressive of the creative flame or the winged dance of desire, but of emotional and human impulses, of desolation, obstinacy, radiance, and so on, qualities to be found in innumerable works of art by men less cloistered than he. Furthermore his music displays, at its best, that perfection of form wherein not a note is wasted, a quality of the utmost rarity in music to which the label romantic, even ultra-romantic, has been attached. Brevity, concentration and understatement inform his best works. They are uncompromising in spirit and in style, and always utterly contemporary. His affected, flamboyant personality attracted the accusation that he was a poseur, fashionable for the sake of fashion alone, but his music contradicts this since it has none of the easy gait of fashionable music of any period. Again, it has been dismissed as mechanical and contrived, but analysis and the fact of its continual stylistic development invalidate the charge.

The later music could never have come into being without the propulsion of a powerfully self-seeking personality (a fact which we have also to observe in the case of Wagner). But if it evokes nothing but that quixotic personality, its message will be unwelcome. If, however, we seize the advantage that music more than any other art possesses, of allowing our own imagination and sensitivity to act in place of his, the music will proclaim its own unquenchable life, independent and sturdy, outliving its creator and aspiring to that immortality to which he imagined he alone had the key.

ORCHESTRAL WORKS

		Opus
1896	Symphonic Allegro	—
1896	Piano Concerto	20
1898	Reverie	24
1899–1900	First Symphony	26
1901	Second Symphony	29
1902–4	Third Symphony: the Divine Poem	43
1905–8	The Poem of Ecstasy	54
1908–10	Prometheus, Poem of Fire	60

PIANO WORKS

1883	Canon	—
1884	Nocturne in A♭	—
1885	Waltz in F minor	1
1886	Sonata-Fantasy	—
1886	Waltz in G♯ minor	—
1886	Waltz in D♭	—
1887	Variations on a theme by Mlle Egorova	—
1889?	Mazurka in F	—
1889?	Mazurka in B minor	—
1889	Albumleaf in A♭	—
1887–9	Sonata in E♭ minor	—
1887–9	3 Pieces	2
1889?	Fantasy (for two pianos)	—
1889	10 Mazurkas	3
1892	Allegro Appassionato	4
1890	2 Nocturnes	5
1892	First Sonata	6
1892	2 Impromptus à la Mazur	7
1894	12 Studies	8
1894	2 Pieces (for the left hand)	9
	1. Prelude 2. Nocturne	
1894	2 Impromptus	10
1888–96	24 Preludes	11
1895	2 Impromptus	12
1895	6 Preludes	13
1895	2 Impromptus	14
1895–6	5 Preludes	15
1894–5	5 Preludes	16
1895–6	7 Preludes	17

The purpose of the series *Oxford Studies of Composers* is to provide short, scholarly, critical surveys of composers about whom no major work is already available, or whose music is in need of re-assessment. The emphasis is on the music itself, biographical data being kept to a minimum.

Skryabin, a composer of great originality saved from probable madness only by his early death, was the leading younger Russian composer of the early years of this century, and an important figure in the final stages of late romantic music. This comprehensive analysis of the music is an invaluable complement to the several biographical studies currently available.

Other books in the series

DEBUSSY
Roger Nichols

GIOVANNI GABRIELI
Denis Arnold

HINDEMITH
Ian Kemp

IVES
H. Wiley Hitchcock

MACHAUT
Gilbert Reaney

MARENZIO
Denis Arnold

MESSIAEN
Roger Nichols

PALESTRINA
Jerome Roche

SCHOENBERG
Anthony Payne

SHOSTAKOVICH
Norman Kay

TALLIS
Paul Doe

WILBYE
David Brown

£2.95 *net in* U.K.

OXFORD UNIVERSITY PRESS
ISBN 0 19 315438 2

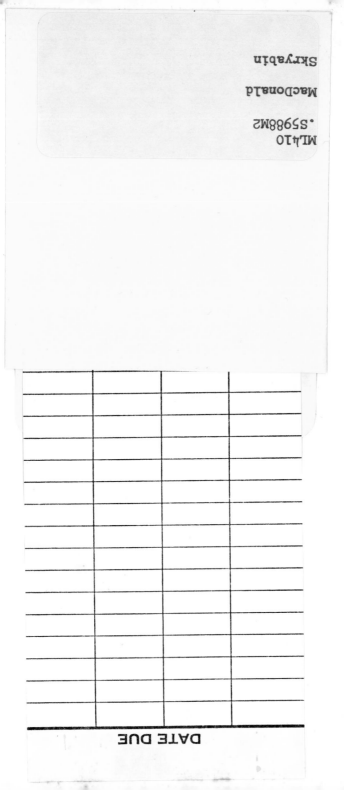

ML410
.S5988M2

MacDonald

Skryabin

DATE DUE